33 by 3:

33 Prompts, 3 Poets, 99 Poems

. . . .

Jacquie Bellon • Liz Collins • Kate Dwyer

Inner Thicket Press

33 by 3
copyright 2020 © Jacquie Bellon, Liz Collins, Kate Dwyer

ISBN # 978-0-578-63039-7
Inner Thicket Press
Nevada City, CA
innerthicket@gmail.com

Cover art: Liz Collins (mixed media)
Book & Cover Design: Julie Valin,
Self to Shelf Publishing.com

All rights reserved.
Printed in the United States of America.
No part of this book may be reproduced in any manner without written permission, except in the use of brief quotations included in critical essays, reviews and articles.

"I read poetry to save time."
–Marilyn Monroe

Foreword

Three poets. Thirty-three prompts. Ninety-nine poems.

The Poets: Jacquie Bellon, Liz Collins, and Kate Dwyer have been writing together for twenty-some odd years. Three good friends with three distinct voices.

The Prompt: A few words or a phrase chosen by one of us on any given day. It is not a topic, rather a starting place. The prompt can lead you anywhere, to the past, to the future, to the world around you and in you. Any style, any length.

The Poems: We learned about "a poem a day" from our friend, the poet Molly Fisk. We pick a prompt a day for a week (or two or four) and write a poem each day with a new prompt. Ten years of this and you have a pile of paper destined for trash or treasure. Then the sifting begins. The poems and prompts are winnowed, trimmed, or tossed, staying true to the basic bones and inspiration.

Table of Prompts

1. How to Start a Poem 9
2. Here's Where It Starts 12
3. Parents as Lovers 15
4. The Back Door 18
5. What We Thought Was Normal 21
6. How We Are Like Our Mothers 24
7. Lipstick 27
8. My Mother's Closet 30
9. Go the Back Way 33
10. Uncertainty 38
11. Devotion 41
12. Shoes 44
13. Spirit Guide 47
14. Accessories 52
15. Hands 55
16. What Kind of Love Are You Talking About? 59
17. You Can't Take It Back 63
18. Remember What I Told You 66
19. Being Useful 69
20. Feel Free 72
21. Why Can't You Just be Happy? 75
22. Should You? 78
23. Forget It 81
24. Collage of the Brain 85

25.	Crossing the Line	89
26.	Assisted Living	94
27.	Other Wise	97
28.	Red Prairie Dawn	100
29.	Just One Tree	103
30.	Wet and Wild Spring	106
31.	Before You Know It	109
32.	If Something Happens to Me	113
33.	In the End	116

Prompt # 1

How to Start a Poem

RECIPE FOR WRITING POEMS

Jacquie Bellon

Throw a handful of words into mixing bowl.
Moisten with equal portions of
lies, longing, lust.
Slowly add a pinch of doubt,
fear, and suffering.
Fold thoroughly then
drape with cloth,
let ferment in warm place.
When mix has
doubled in size,
scoop out a teaspoon full,
throw rest away.
Feed new brew with
truth, beauty and love,
let ferment in cool place.
When mix has
doubled in size,
scoop out a teaspoon full,
throw rest away.
Run fingers through,
roll what clings into little
balls and toss against a wall.
Whatever sticks
is ready to rise,
becoming firmer
to withstand slashing
with a double-edged razor
for a lacerating crust,
but supple enough for an
open textured tender crumb
after baking in a 500 degree oven.

Prompt #1: How to Start a Poem

STARTING A POEM

Liz Collins

spill it all
dump it out
like engine parts
there's no sense
wait for movement
the earth to heave
an inhale
parts tumble here
and there
and out of the waiting

a delicate sprout wends its way
through piles
and sometimes a bud will form
petals will unfurl
a surprise
the thing
you've been waiting for.

Prompt #1: How to Start a Poem

How to Start a Poem

Kate Dwyer

You need a reason:
you wish you could kill someone
or your heart is pierced
with betrayal, with unspeakable beauty,
with some gale force emotion
pitching you headlong into it.

Don't have a reason:
it's stifling.
You'll be trapped,
like that mouse in the dryer vent.
Just open to a fresh page,
feel the breeze behind your ears.

Prompt # 2

Here's Where It Starts

My mother #1

Jacquie Bellon

Started out a natural
blonde, more on
the dark side
of blonde.
As she grew older
her hair got lighter
until she went
platinum all
the way to
her death.

Prompt #2: Here's Where It Starts

Blue Dress

Liz Collins

It's not her fault,
who she became to me.
It's the paper mâché of memory
the way we slap another wet piece
over the last, the heavier pieces
showing through to the end
like the one where she grabbed
my hair, wrestled me to the ground.

I built her up early on
layer by starchy layer
chain-smoking, "V" browed
discontent and it's hard
to change direction after a bad start
this sculpture, this mother,
to Madonna.

And now, as if the tip of her blue sleeve
poked through trampled earth like a flower
the song comes, "Shall We Dance?"
she, singing her happiness
pure, the color of ancient sky
before my thousand troops
marched her under, before unskilled hands
pressed a false figure.

I want to pull that bit of sleeve
unearth what I've covered
I want the whole blue dress
with its fleur de lis pattern the joy
of brass buttons down the back

I want to pick around her truth
like an archeologist
pull up the bones
of her happiness, mold her anew
let her teach me to waltz.
I want to hear the whole song.

Prompt #2: Here's Where It Starts

Church

Kate Dwyer

On Sunday mornings he sat at the piano
cigarette loosely poised between his lips
and played an ambling boogie woogie
while we dressed for church.
How was it he always finished first?
His suit on, his tie tied, his shiny
oxfords glistening on the pedals.
Meanwhile, upstairs, I challenged
why God needed me to wear a dress,
my sister dawdled, distracted by her trolls,
and my brother refused to rise at all.
My mother's heels clicked up and down the halls,
in and out of bedrooms
while his walking bass line
matched her beat for beat.
Eventually three pair of Sunday shoes
would trudge down the stairs, gather at the piano,
resigned to their fate.
My father's head would turn,
cigarette bobbing as he studied us
head to toe, left to right,
confirming we were indeed ready.
All the while hands still playing
his rolling Sunday Morning Blues.

Prompt # 3

Parents as Lovers

My Mother #2

Jacquie Bellon

A lifetime of high heels
condemned her tendons,
diet pills, face lifts, girdles, corsets,
pantyhose, perfume, cigarettes,
all in the service of beauty.
Bedridden in her eighties,
still blonde, nearly blind she'd
paint her eyelids, lips,
missing the boundaries.
All of this
for my father's love.

Prompt #3: Parents as Lovers

DISARMAMENT

Liz Collins

If he could have looked her in the eye
if she could have seen, there,
beyond her reflection, the scarred landscape
the clearcutting of his pride
if they could have pressed palm to palm
explored for a few crucial seconds
the skin of old love
spoken niceties
for the sake of possibility

or if she could have reached over the line
pulled my father's hand
that simple gesture that subtle move into his corner
--while making the Gibsons perhaps—
her hand her fingers lightly brushing his
could have made all the difference.

Prompt #3: Parents as Lovers

DAUPHIN ISLAND, 1964

Kate Dwyer

It's a Kodak beach at sunset.
He's tall, curly black hair, blue checked shirt,
tucked into cream trousers,
rolled up to his calves.
He's holding shoes in one hand,
his wife's hand in the other.
She's in a skirt,
red sleeveless blouse, with
her hair in a kerchief.
Their heads are tilting towards each other,
so she can hear his plans for their life
over the sound of gentle waves
rolling onto the beach.
They are walking away from the camera
towards the sun just now
touching the horizon.

He will win an election in 1 year
and leave banking.
He will begin his affair in 2 years,
lose an election in 3,
start a business in 4.
Their marriage will end in 7 years.

Tonight, though, they are poetry.
They are exactly why Midwesterners
drive 16 hours to the gulf coast,
to watch the same sun
they have back home
and ignore, as it
dips below the horizon
and disappears.

Prompt # 4

The Back Door

THE BACK DOOR

Jacquie Bellon

That was where
I kept my foot
during much of
the marriage,
thinking I'd get out
first before him.
The front door
didn't close anymore
It'd been slammed
so many times.

Prompt #4: The Back Door

No Words

Liz Collins

You don't have to be old or wise
to know Something Big.

At eight I knew the meaning
of infinity--it landed on me like a bomb
an explosion of nothingness, no words.

I waited. Maybe words would come with age.
I searched the dictionary. No words to explain
what I knew. No colors, it wasn't a soft blue hue.
Nothing to draw. Arrows could point
to unfathomable distance, but distance
suggested an end point. No words.
If you don't have words
then you don't know.
But I knew.
I knew in a back-door sort of way
Something Big, afraid
to call it God.

Prompt #4: The Back Door

URBANA ILLINOIS, 1933

Kate Dwyer

Back then, my mother said, men
would come to the side of the house,
knock on the shingles, ask for
work they could do for a sandwich
or a bowl of beans.
Silent and aproned, Grandma
would listen, screen door ajar,
then give them a task.
Stack those boards.
Wash this tub out.
Coil that rope there.
Meanwhile, she served a meal
fit for company, at a little table
right outside the door.
My mother said Grandad thought
there must be chalked arrows
out there on that sidewalk somewhere
guides them all the way
from the rail yards.
And yet, my mother said,
he always left a chore right there
where you couldn't miss it,
just beyond the back door.

Prompt # 5

What We Thought Was Normal

WHAT WE THOUGHT WAS NORMAL
Jacquie Bellon

Not so long ago
when the oak leaves were
the size of squirrel's ears
we'd plant a garden,
note that the wise apple
would not bloom until
all danger of frost,
of deluvian rains
was past. But now
there's an urgency,
a rush to bloom, to seed.
Even the rain is trying hard.
We're all doing
our best to stay viable,
keep a balance while
spinning out of control.
Maybe a superbloom will
drop enough seeds for
the future shrinking before
our eyes wide open.

Prompt #5: What We Thought Was Normal

NOT FOR GIRLS

Liz Collins

From afar you might have seen
our New Jersey home pulsing throbbing
pressing the seams like a ruined heart

that house a pressure cooker
of sharp shards a stew
of mother daughter wounds.

I thought it was normal the fighting
that's how girls were strong in the world
hold your fist to the wind

fight for what you believe
no matter how small is how she did it
how I should do it

"That boy" she'd say "why is your hair what kind of skirt who is that girl"
she'd say "why can't you be like"
but I was not like them good like them

I fought like I was taught a girl should fight
no quiet for me no holding back
like my father
looking up and over
the tops of oblong glasses.

What We Thought Was Normal
Kate Dwyer

Potable water,
lights that turn on,
food that nourishes,
a doctor for ailments,
safe passage to hither or yon
and back again,
money for bills
and a little left over
for peace of mind.

From this side of the moat
it seems a modest list.
Who would accept less?
From that side of the moat
it's a dream, now fierce and tantalizing,
now far away, dully impossible.

From this side of the moat
a bomb in a market
is so inconceivable
that some imagine
a pistol on everyone's hip
could prevent it.

On that side of the moat
a father with a loaded
machine gun in every room
of his family's house,
knows better.

On that side of the moat
loss and more loss is normal.
Abundance in all things
is a gift from God
only to the mighty.

Prompt # 6

How We Are Like Our Mothers

MALLOU

Jacquie Bellon

She was blond,
loud, vain. She loved
tinsel, glitter, artifice,
fame, Hollywood.
She loved me.
I set myself apart,
how unlike her
I might become.
I walked the other way.
But when it came
to love she
revealed a landscape
without borders & frontiers.
I lurched, stumbled on the path
she had traveled,
picked my way through
ruts and stubble
and found that point
of ecstasy she wanted
me to feel.

Prompt #6: How We Are Like Our Mothers

GENETICS

Liz Collins

The way I have always been able to sit
even as a child
and stare out the window
at nothing, the way you can just give it all up.

"Ma," I'd say and hold her chin
between my first three fingers,
turn her abandoned face toward mine.
Sometimes her eyes would stay behind.
"Did you hear what I said?"
I didn't want her to give it all up
not me anyway.

But now I know what it's like
you lay your mind down
let it spread like a lake
calm, reflecting, no ripple of thought
it's like a breath in the chaos
an open field in the jungle
"Ma," my own daughter says
"Did you hear what I said?"

Prompt #6: How We Are Like Our Mothers

THE CRACK IN THE MIRROR

Kate Dwyer

It is the Divine Comedy,
Moby Dick with footnotes,
Pilgrim's Progress in old English.
Entangled and complex,
there are one hundred thousand ways
I am like my mother.
They are profound,
embarrassingly obvious,
veiled and tender.
Every saved shard,
every overextended loyalty,
every obligation fulfilled,
every patient listening,
every solitary raking of the leaves;
the one hundred thousand ways
are in every breath.
But the haiku
of how I am not
takes my breath away.

Prompt # 7

Lipstick

GRANDDAUGHTER

Jacquie Bellon

At eleven she's allowed
lip gloss—a shear sheen
slicked on her pink lips.
She's getting ready for lipstick,
seduction with its
hard edges and molten core,
the exploration of kisses
beyond the ones we plant
on her cheeks, her head.
I tremble for her.

Prompt #7: Lipstick

SHE DRESSES UP

Liz Collins

my mother
leans in to the mirror
parts her lips midlife pale
tightens them and paints
Poppy Red by Merle Norman
deftly on her upper
pressing it up and around
a lower case "m"
she swipes right from midline then left
the transformation quick and dramatic

at her side I follow her movements
with my mouth
the way a mother's mouth mimics
her spoon-fed baby

she is not about sexy
she is about business
motherhood
household chores
but what do I know at ten?
she is my mother and she wears
a red jacket to match her lips
sometimes a red skirt
or heels with a touch
of Merle Norman red

she is not going anywhere
but downstairs
to the kitchen
to fix dinner
dressed to the nines

my father leans back at the table
under a lamp drinking a Gibson
the kind with an onion.

LIPSTICK

Kate Dwyer

To remind my co-workers of my
sophisticated business acumen
I would wear a chestnut mauve lipstick
to work. Touch it up on break
and after lunch.
Summer Saturday mornings,
there at the farmer's market,
maybe a frosty peachy pink.
Everyone shows up so rested and rosy,
and those young farmers, well, they're young.
At night, I'd choose my richest, reddest red.
One fat glossy sweep across the bottom lip,
then top center swipe right,
swipe left.
Voila! Beauty.
But I don't wear lipstick.
It tastes noxious.
It gets on people's faces when I kiss them,
smears wine glasses when I drink.
At memorials, after the tissue is soaked,
my sleeves are wet with little red blotches.
Most of all, with glossy red lips
I look 5 times better than I feel.
So it's chap-stick for me
and truth in advertising.

Prompt # 8

My Mother's Closet

MY MOTHER'S CLOSET

Jacquie Bellon

Beyond the usual
her closet held
the dead baby,
my brother's father,
the successive husbands, lovers,
my father's lovers,
my adoption altered
by magical thinking.
Over a lifetime she
would pull an item
and startle me with
its edited content.
When I emptied her closet
I found bones,
discarded masks,
nothing useful left.

Prompt #8: My Mother's Closet

MY MOTHERS CLOSET

Liz Collins

It was the first thing I'd do
after dropping my books on the floor
and racing to pee,
I'd seek her out.
I liked to find her asleep
on the sofa her cheek
imprinted with dreams
and the pillow's rough weave.

When she'd wake slowly to see me
standing there she wouldn't linger
but busy herself with dinner.
Or something else.

Her closet was where I looked
if she was not there
on the sofa. I reasoned
if her shoes were there
so was she.
Flinging its doors wide
I would expect to find it empty
feared that she would be gone.

But there they always were
her shoes, the reds
the blues, creams, grays,
the two tones,
the party of them
all those happy shoes.

My Mother's Closet, 1932-1940

Kate Dwyer

It was a drawer in the hall
just outside the kitchen.
Dishes above, linens below.
One drawer for a few
dresses and knee socks,
blouses and panties.
She slept on a pallet, unrolled
after the evening meal,
after the crossword puzzle,
under the kitchen table.
What about toys? I asked.
What about a room?
What about privacy
and your own bed?
Where did you hang
a coat, or an ironed dress?
"Oh I forgot", she smiled,
savoring a delicious memory.
"I had a hook on the back of
the bathroom door.
It was just for me,
just for things like that."

Prompt # 9

Go the Back Way

GAS, FOOD, LODGING

Jacquie Bellon

Press on past the sign
deeper into desert,
only two lanes now
and no lights
for miles.
Pick a dirt road,
raise a little dust,
find a Juniper tree
big enough to hide the car.
Step out
into the night,
let the silence
silence you,
the stars define space.
Lay your body down
become still now.

Prompt #9: Go the Back Way

BUTLER, NEW JERSEY 1965

Liz Collins

She liked to go the back way to Butler
not route 23 the two-lane highway
but the winding and long, hilly way
and I liked this altered route in the spring
just after a rain when the green was so much
so full so lush it rolled
down to the road
engulfing the curves swallowing
houses to the peak of a roof
the edge of a shack up a drive
where deer parts
hung on clotheslines.

I'd press my face
to the back-seat window,
wishing it did not lay between
me and the exotic
the rough and tumble
of Butler where my mother went
to buy fish, hem a dress,
order a vacuum.

Our Grand Prix Oldsmobile
floated Main Street
like Queen Elizabeth
touring the south Bronx.

Eye shadowed eighth graders
hung on corners
with slick backed boys
and from behind the windshield
homework in lap I studied
their swivel and swoop.

Prompt #9: Go the Back Way

I wanted it all; their old wrecked cars and leather jackets
their "D"s their "F"s their empty notebooks
for margin-scribbled love
I wanted their sex
I wanted their tough,
the raw and real, the hard life
I imagined as freedom.

But when my mother
finished the things
she could not do in our town
we would wind our way
back through the lush green
world of rambling shacks
that somehow pushed
against all I was taught
to be true.

We drove on
without speech
to our house
starched and white
up the mountain road.

Prompt #9: Go the Back Way

Go the Back Way

Kate Dwyer

There is a faster way,
a four lane version.
But you'll miss the wild dogwood,
the hillsides of lupine and poppy
against those black basalt boulders.
You'll miss the river crossing
where looking left
the canyon falls away
and the valley opens up.
Look right and there's that pasture
with the Texas Longhorns
in knee high grass.
They barely crick their necks
to scratch an itch on a hip
with those luxurious horns of theirs.

You could just take the Interstate.
It's simpler.
The road's resurfaced;
bright anodized guard rails
along newly engineered
50mph curves.
You'll be there in no time.
But you'll miss that little store
with fresh homemade
key lime pie to die for,
and that old iron yard,
impossible to drive past
without stopping.

Prompt #9: Go the Back Way

Tall grass growing through
ornate gates and railings,
weathervanes leaning
this way and that,
almost beyond wanting
a home of their own.
See that's it:
go the back way and
who knows when you'll show up.

Prompt # 10

Uncertainty

PERMISSION

Jacquie Bellon

You can do whatever you want,
nothing is wasted,
everything matters,
nothing matters.
Start knowing for sure
exactly nothing.

Prompt #10: Uncertainty

AN IMMACULATE DEATH

Liz Collins

I've been two days
scanning the sky for buzzards.

Where he once lay are now just flies
as if his body morphed into the swarm.
I must move the tan dog pillow
it startles me each time I see it
thinking he's come home.

His brother's ears twitch
his eyes scan the canyon
of downed beetle-kill
from which he may see a sign.
For hours he sits there
waiting.

Wherever he sniffs, I sleuth
scuffle marks? paw prints? blood?
coyotes and mountain lions prey on the weak
but nothing.

It's like he was plucked from the land
while no one was looking, beamed
up to a ship in the sky.
He couldn't walk far
with four bad legs
he is nowhere.

Yet I feel him. In whatever form I feel him.
And I only know for certain he is gone
when the silence is full enough
and the air is humid with his presence.

UNCERTAINTY

Kate Dwyer

How shall my demise unfold?
Let me count the ways.
Fiscal ruin under the watchful eye
of my glossy financial planner.
Perhaps the cancer du jour
sapping health and savings
all in one tidy stroke.
An online weasel tapping into
every password created, ravaging
identity, credit, reputation.
Gigolo Extraordinaire whispering the words
not even imagined for decades,
breaking both my heart and home.
Global pandemic, jihad upon the homeland,
accidental toxic spill, precision nuclear warhead,
mega fire sweeping the landscape,
machine gun fire spraying the farmer's market.
Have I left something out?
Let me turn on the news to check.
Life is short, death looms, and hope seems entangled
on the latch of Pandora's box.

Prompt # 11

Devotion

Fall Soup

Jacquie Bellon

He makes a thick soup
from the fall harvest.
To the avalanche of cut up
carrots, leeks, squash, leafy greens,
he adds rice, lentils, kelp, a dash of soy.
This he stirs with
his sweet heart, his goodwill, his delight
in the lavish use of
everything good and simple.
Did I say it right?
what I really meant to say
is how like the soup he is,
nourishing, deeply satisfying, surprisingly complex.
And in the next days
becoming richer, deeper, more concentrated,
so that with every
mouthful comes a sigh of relief,
a letting go into simply being.

Prompt #11: Devotion

THE COMMISSION
Liz Collins

She came to my studio,
spirited in from the rain
bolstered by friends
who kept the room light
and her story afloat
she filled my studio
with her husband, a genie
from a bottle, his large love
her real and unencumbered devotion.

I wasn't prepared
paper towels all I could offer
her rims still red after months yet
with the sparkle of remembering.
It was all there, laughter not denied.

Her friends floated through my studio
one ear to the story, ready to prop her up
"And should you tell her about Valentine's Day?" and
"What about the muffins?"
so I heard it all, his Irish heritage and addiction,
40 years sober and hep C
his new liver, the cure which—who knew--
did not pair with foreign parts, this
a tiny peek
into a large man.

I can only try
to grant her wish
to push the newly rain-soaked seed
to bud on my brush, to alight
a tint of his essence.

Devotion

Kate Dwyer

A forest green canopy
provides no shelter
from the rain blowing sideways.
The token pile of dirt
beside the open grave
is mud. Tossed onto the casket
it will not crumble poetically, it will thwack.
Still the mourners have come,
a small but stalwart huddle of black.
Umbrellas gripped with two hands
against the wind over the widow,
touchingly ineffective.

Up the way, standing under the eaves
of the cemetery tool shed
is the bulldozer driver and his
two helpers. They're smoking,
immune to both the weather and the grief,
well trained to wait
for the last pair of soaked
black shoulders to fold into a car
and drive away.

Prompt # 12

Shoes

PROCRASTINATION

Jacquie Bellon

You don't wanna'
be in my
shabby chic shoes.
They're full of burrs,
velcro seeds waiting
to be scattered
if only they'd
let go while,
I pace in place
shifting stance
going nowhere
fast.

Prompt #12: Shoes

At the Museum

Liz Collins

Pointed toes round toes white and shiny saddle shoes
ankle boots and patterned tights pink and patent leather
beige with buckles laces tied dirty muddy there's a penny
in a loafer pant cuffs and petticoats
black and scalloped wing tips tapping stepping
twisting skirt hems flowered plain
her shoes are red
his are black
both are gone

lost-
in an underworld of abstract art
a blur of blacks and whites and darkened colors
her cry is muted, jostled
in the din

but an arm
reaches through
scoops her up
she crashes through
the ceiling of shirt sleeves
and coats into the light and air
colors heightened
and faces, oh those faces
and her tears rest soft
on a whiskered cheek.

Prompt #12: Shoes

Ciao Bella

Kate Dwyer

She sent a box of shoes.
Sublime Italian ankle boots,
Sienna brown.
Leather so soft I just
wanted to set one in my lap
and stroke it with my thumb.
It took her 6 months to pay them off.
A sunny shop on Via Condotti,
just off the Spanish Steps.
That was decades ago, and
now they're here in my kitchen
atop the wood stove, afternoon sun
catching the edge of timeless 1 1/2 inch heels.
I can't imagine where I'd be going
standing in these shoes,
what the rest of me would be wearing.
Would I be glad I'd gone afterwards,
sitting there on the edge of the bed,
unlacing my elegant boots
and setting them tenderly
back in their box?

Prompt # 13

Spirit Guide

E<small>ARL</small>

Jacquie Bellon

I've always had cats.
They all disappeared
the way they came,
mysteriously,
except for Earl
son of Lorca.
Lorca wandered in one day
pregnant and barefoot.
When she and her kittens
were adopted by friends
Earl stayed and ruled.
He was an attractive, charming,
red head, a big game hunter
stalking turkeys and deer.
When the ex left
Earl slept close to
my chest and purred.
At 50 hertz
The vibration
strengthened bones,
muscles, tendons, ligaments,
healed my weeping wound,
my broken heart,
until I could stand alone.
And then he disappeared
like all the others
whose names I've forgotten.

Prompt #13: Spirit Guide

Emissaries

Liz Collins

She campaigned for my attention
with the zest of colored confetti
flitting and chirping on the low branch
and it was perfectly clear *who* the bird was
even if the message was not.
The message never is.

It's more like a waving from the other side
like "Hey. Made it so far. Seem to be in some kind of limbo
wish you were here
or I was there, or something."

Even though I waited patiently
for the message in the Sanskrit of birdsong
hidden behind the confessional's cloth
separating the living from the dead
all I got was the waving,
"hi, it's me" kinda thing.

Yes, I'm certain it was Carol
come to say her final goodbyes
in the body of a bird and all I can think is
why don't they just come back as themselves?
Why is it always a bird, or a cat, or a moth?
Or why not even some other human?
If Carol say, came back as Richard III
then we'd know for sure it was her
for one, because he could say so, for two, because
who else would it be
two days post death?

If you all think I'm crazy
when Doris died her group of friends
all felt her flash on the horizon, one green second
I missed it.

But at two a.m. my bedroom light turned on
of its own, Doris not one to leave me out.

Prompt #13: Spirit Guide

Heather claims a barking owl with the death of her dog
and there's the moth who arrived mid-winter
flattening itself on Samantha's screen door
angel wings spread wide availing itself
to her house-sized grief, her husband gone
we all gathered on the inside,
witnessing through the screen its heart belly.

When I die
and if the rules say I can't
say my final goodbyes as a human
then wouldn't it be more dramatic to make it big
come back as say, a Pterodactyl?
I'm sure there are rules I don't know about
but it *is* a winged thing
which seems to be preferred.

Maybe it has to be small, maybe the loved ones
need to look hard to prove
their devotion and despair one final time
maybe it's a game like Where's Waldo
if so, I'll be peeking out from behind
the portrait on the wall.
I'll be waving,
if that's allowed.

I'm hoping I could be something like
snow falling in July, some kind of miracle
that everyone sees at once
so I don't have to show up separately
pestering for each person's attention
banging my beak on their window
or crawling my little ant feet
in the form of their initials on the wall
and what if I forget someone?

I get the feeling I'll be in a hurry
so just a heads-up
there may not be time for all of you.

Prompt #13: Spirit Guide

Divorce: A Canine Perspective

Kate Dwyer

Well, it's no dog park.
The blind-to-the-world, flailing-on-the-floor grief
you wait through, standing unseen
at the back door, needing to go out.
Her head's down, eyes unfocused.
Even if there was a dog door,
could you leave her now?

Eating is sporadic.
She's not hungry.
She thinks caring for you
keeps her grounded.
Eye level with her knees, standing over your empty bowl,
clearly only your feet feel the floor.

Walks, though,
are timeless, and that's sweet.
There's no place to go, no one to see.
You lead the way, she follows like a sleepy child.
And you can stand,
peeling open a fragrance one layer at a time
for as long as you like.
When you're done, you gently tug on the leash,
and she stumbles behind,
grateful for direction.

Nights, though, are interminable.
The bed too soft, blankets too hot.
She grips your shoulders,
cries in your neck,
and you look away,
as any polite predator would.
She forgets she's the shepherd.
She forgets you're a dog.

Prompt #13: Spirit Guide

And she weeps for a man
who smelled sour from the beginning.
She clasps you, asks for loving eyes,
and you hope loyal will do.
You wait for her hold to loosen
so you can drop to the cool floor
and just be a dog
on a rug, sleeping.

Prompt # 14

Accessories

STEVE'S KNIFE

Jacquie Bellon

Swift and sharp
it merely stung
slicing through flesh and nail
down to almost bone.
I felt warm
blood sluicing through
pressed together fingers,
a slippery trail
to bathroom sink.
Looked away while
he flushed, cleaned,
sterilized, bandaged,
talked down the shock,
"ugliest thing
I've ever seen" he said.

The green onion
big as my finger,
fragrant.

Prompt #14: Accessories

THE BRACELET

Liz Collins

meant she was taken
chain and silver worn low on her wrist
cascading grand and wide as Niagara Falls
over her smooth young hand
there for the world to see
his name," Doug" inscribed
yes, she was somebody's-
protected and possessed.

Secretly she fingers the nameplate
below the tabletop
her mother does not look at her
her father asks of homework
her fingers Braille the etched crevasses
four letters like eggs in the nest
of her lap and she wants to say see,
this is how I will be loved

I am taken, no longer yours.

Prompt #14: Accessories

SWISS ARMY KNIFE

Kate Dwyer

The Mont Blanc model;
Scissors, awl, tweezers
3 kinds of screw drivers,
Leather punch, saw,
pressed white shirt,
black trousers and
cufflinks; everything
you need and then some.

On the way to dinner
the car has a flat.
The jack is broken,
so he repairs it with
a coat hanger, then
changes the tire,
all while whistling.
Tomorrow he will
drop the tire off
for repair
on his way to work.
You won't have to ask.

Arriving at dinner only
fashionably late,
he charms your friends,
pours your champagne,
joins any conversation,
nano-tech, constitutional law,
sauerkraut recipes,
all after checking
with the hostess-
does she need him
to make gravy?
Tell me you realize
a good pocket knife is
worth its weight in gold.

Prompt # 15

Hands

A NUDE MODEL EVERY SATURDAY

Jacquie Bellon

What my mind knows
is not what it sees.
What the mind sees
my hands try to translate
with pencil to paper.
But the mind persists,
invents muscles & bones,
a face with nostrils
like bullet holes.
When I get to the hands
I count the fingers,
especially when interlaced.
Draw popsicle toes after
fudging around the ankles.
It's hard-I'll never get it right,
So many moving parts,
I have to lie a little bit.
Just to be convincing.

Prompt #15: Hands

Right Hand's Missive to the Left

Liz Collins

I can't say I'm not burdened, I mean look at me
stubby, dirty, blue-collar nails, hambone knuckles
I do it all pretty much, the chopping
brushing, writing, even the thinking
when the missus leaves it up to me.

Heck! I do most of the driving
'cept when the missus wants me to feed her blueberries
or make her cheese and crackers in the car
which I will do no longer since your driving
is far from excellent.

But I see you there, don't think I don't,
lying on her lap daydreaming
or pretending to hold the paper
while I'm sweating from writing so hard
or sometimes you just slump over
the fork while I saw away at the meat
like you have no pride in your job
and that's the kind of thing that's getting to me lately.

Even though you were always prettier than me
neither of us have ever been much to look at
why, even when we were young and plump
we hid in our kindergarten pockets
shied from holding hands.

But there was a short period,
remember, when we were proud of our working class look
and when the missus would exclaim, "Oh!"
or be listening with a serious face
we took every opportunity to jump up
cover her mouth in her excitement, or feel her face
just to be seen, remember? As if we were flashing

Prompt #15: Hands

a big diamond rock to the world,
when it was just us, two roughhewn
laquer-thinnered hands of an artist
proud to work in the dirt, the paint
to hold drills and hammers and mat knives.

I know you always wanted a different look than me
and I gotta say way back you woulda looked mighty pretty
in long pink nails but that's not what we were born into
and when I did slip that ring on your finger at the jeweler's
for the first time and you wanted the smallest diamond
you were the most beautiful then
and now that I'm semi-retired and you're still retired,
I just like that we hold hands
or lie side by side in the missus' lap
rubbing our knuckles or whatever.

Prompt #15: Hands

What Are You Holding Onto?

Kate Dwyer

I know one pair of hands
better than my own,
have been enamored of them for years.
I forget to have eye contact
while watching them peel apples,
de-vein shrimp for Pad Thai,
cut bread, fold a linen napkin.
Most of all, I like to watch them
write dense short poems that
kick me in the stomach
with the last line.
The one hand holds a fat fountain pen
as though it just learned how to
write cursive this morning.
The other hand lies atop
one corner of the paper,
as still as a monk's meditation.
Once in a hospital,
I watched the hands sitting vigil.
Thumb stroking skin between
the eyebrows of a dying friend.
When one hand tired,
the other replaced it.
No other solace present
matched the comfort
of those hands.

Prompt # 16

What Kind of Love Are You Talking About?

You Were the Ocean

Jacquie Bellon

You were the ocean
and I was the shore.
Wasn't it like that?
You kept leaving
and coming back.
I stood my ground.
What no one saw
was the embrace,
how we broke
into each other.

Prompt #16: What Kind of Love Are You Talking About?

Faraway Loving

Liz Collins

In late September, we disentangle
from summer's whirl and as
trees emerge golden
from a darkening ground
so do you, once again.

Your large and callused fingers
snap the back of a Barbie Doll pants suit
and from across the room, I am loving you
now bumbling around the kitchen
making a cake with our daughter,
discussing frosting choices and birthday cards.

And when you hold our tiny kitten
in the palm of your strong hand
I hug you from where I sit.

I do this a lot, this faraway loving,
caressing your creased face
kissing your stubbled mouth,

I love you from the garden, the kitchen sink,
from errands in the car
the tips of my faraway fingers love
your thin, black ribbon of belly hair,
and my nose your racy smell
of hardworking sweat.

I forget to tell you
how I've secretly loved you
and when you walk in to the room,
and I am stirring the soup,
I am miserly in real-life loving
as if I've spent it all in a dream.

Prompt #16: What Kind of Love Are You Talking About?

So if my arms don't tell the story
know how I adore the truth
of your real arms encircling me from behind,
your humid breath on my neck and the soft pressing
of your full body against mine.

WHAT KIND OF LOVE ARE YOU TALKING ABOUT?

Kate Dwyer

I'm sorry,
did you say *everlasting*?
I may have, inadvertently,
misrepresented myself.
And *passionate*? On the prairie
passion can get you killed,
usually by frostbite.

Here's what I could offer:
You know that peat moss
up north, underground?
Lightning strikes and it catches
on fire, then smolders invisibly
for 200 years? Nothing burns down.
There isn't even any smoke to speak of-
That's the kind of love
I was talking about.

Prompt # 17

You Can't Take It Back

THE HEART

Jacquie Bellon

You can't take it back
once it's flown from
your rib cage.
It will change,
become enlarged or
broken, desiccated even.
It might perch
on our sleeve awhile,
sing an aria or two,
flutter, attack, or burn.
So let it go
it has work to do.

Prompt #17: You Can't Take It Back

WORDS

Liz Collins

They have fouled
the red carpet of your tongue
made their way to the light of day
flapping and blinking
like baby birds, stunned,
for it was not the plan
to burst out like buckshot
you wanted them to unfurl
like a royal scroll.

But there they lie, all a-jumble
and there's no taking them back
no re-swallowing-- the damage
lives inside the silence—

their essence forever remains
the way atoms of a thing—a house—
merely change to ashes in the fire.

You Can't Take It Back

Kate Dwyer

Thoughts:
In your head they can recycle
for days, for years,
growing, shrinking
morphing, vaporizing,
gone.
But once spoken
there's mass, weight, flesh.
Now they're plastic
and forever. Bury them.
Cut them into tiny strips,
apologize on their behalf; they're still there,
filling space,
changing everything,
most of all,
you.

Prompt # 18

Remember What I Told You

ANSWER ME

Jacquie Bellon

So when I took you
out to lunch
when we said good-bye
when I said
don't die before me
when you promised
so why did you go
and do just that?

Prompt #18: Remember What I Told You

REMEMBER WHEN I TOLD YOU

Liz Collins

Remember when I told you
this was not what I really wanted?
I knew how windswept winters
could turn to summers' drought
how easily a day becomes a year
a year a lifetime.

You cannot blame me, then,
when what you could not spare
arrived as naturally as water
flowing down; my future husband
and infant daughter both at once
and unexpected.

You cannot blame me, then, for leaving.

Remember What You Told Me?

Kate Dwyer

Remember what you told me?
That day we were walking on the beach in
Eastern Maryland?
You said some day
we'll have been happily ever aftering
for 40 years.
Remember what I told you?
Was it in the kitchen or as I followed
you out to the car, sobbing?
It takes years to build a home,
but you can burn it down in a minute.
Are you sure you want to burn this down?
Remember what you told me?
I'm lighting the match.

Prompt # 19

Being Useful

BEING USEFUL

Jacquie Bellon

"When are you leaving?"
my granddaughter asks
on the way home from class.
My presence confirms
that her mother
will not pick her up
from school
anytime soon,
that I show up
when another
run to the ER
happens at 3 A.M.
I'm here when
her mom gets worse.
She wants her life to be
what it was before cancer.
I'm not being useful
I remind her how bad
things really are.

Prompt #19: Being Useful

WALK ON

Liz Collins

My plump heart
could burst with his grief
tenor sorrow singeing his words
no one can replace him, he says,
his beautiful man with a woman's name
rings on every finger a hat
for each occasion, ebony skin and dreadlocks
the smell of ripe persimmons.
I am too old, he says,
eleven years are gone.

There are things I cannot say-
hecklers of grim truth-
and things I can.

Gather your strength
your life's practice
build a fire
incant
be a shaman to your own good self
hold steady and walk on
like it's what you always wanted.

These words he won't hear
I know
I've stood where he stands now
yet still they leave my lips
they're all I know to say.

Being Useful

Kate Dwyer

She is not well traveled.
She has not been to Paris or Berlin,
Cairo or Johannesburg.
She's not a template of high fashion,
no impeccably draped trouser line,
with sweeping silk scarf to frame her face.
She does not wax philosophically
on Rembrandt's self-portraits,
or the merits of free-verse poetry.
She is just about being useful.

It is her vocation and her avocation,
her calling and her cross.
She rises, drinks her coffee, and sets about it.
How can she help? The neighbors,
the man in the park collecting bottles,
the woman who made four critical mistakes in a row and so
lives in a travel trailer at the fairgrounds
in the dead of winter.
Hot coffee, a ride to the grocery,
the listening end of a conversation.
Each receives the full attention
of her practice, the grace
of her observance.

Prompt # 20

Feel Free

INVITATION

Jacquie Bellon

The door opens
there is no key.
Spring water from
the faucet is pure.
Have a glass, have a seat,
take some time,
and do nothing.
Feel free to
just be here.

Prompt #20: Feel Free

Feel Free

Liz Collins

Feel free to try it on
the saleswoman says dangling
the Maidenform bra
size 27 AAA mid store
might as well have been doing the can-can
on a spotlighted stage
my bra as the boa.

She and my mother, conspirators
smile knowingly at all within earshot
I blend and freeze
I am a mannequin.

I sweat in the dressing room
plan how I will tear off
my pink Felix the Cat shirt
dive into the item
carefully laid out before me
in one quick spurt

and she is there
her glasses inches
from my bony white torso
Everything fit? Size OK?
Do your bosoms fill the cups?
She doesn't even know me
and she's using the word bosom
the unspeakable word of which
I have none.

Sweat is dripping
from newly dark underarms
and suddenly I know I've arrived
in a foreign country
with no ticket home.

Prompt #20: Feel Free

The Back-up Plan

Kate Dwyer

I tell everyone "Barista". I say
barista, but secretly I'm thinking
Pony Express.
Cantering that sure-footed
brown mare of mine through the dew,
leather mail pouch slapping against my back.
Love, money, news from home-
all delivered at a gallop.
Whose face wouldn't light up
to see us crest the hill,
cutting through the tall grass like wind?
Mother, put the coffee
on the stove.
Mail's a comin'.

Prompt # 21

Why Can't You Just be Happy?

Why Can't you just be Happy?

Jacquie Bellon

So what if
he drank too much,
was gone a lot,
couldn't communicate.
He fucked your brains out,
made you laugh,
designed and built
the house by hand,
took you down
wild and scenic rivers,
raised your boy.

So what if
he got stoned,
roared with rage,
threw you across
the room once,
made you a beggar in
the house of love.
So why couldn't you
just be happy?

Prompt #21: Why Can't You Just be Happy?

THE WAY IT GOES
Liz Collins

Before the deaths and the accident,
before the friend turned foe, and the bigger things
there were little things, the bounced checks
and burnt casseroles, the plate against the wall
plenty of things
to put a stain on love.

I remember the beginning
how you tipped my chin
to meet your stubbled mouth in the snow
the fog of our breath lifting,
I felt then this love rising
in my chest like good bread.
I thought it would rise forever.

Now I know you through the phone.
I call you in my boredom on the road
on the way to far places.
Before I speak you say,
You're on the road and I say *yeah*
And its ok that I call you this way. We talk for an hour
sometimes three, that bread still rising.

WHY CAN'T YOU JUST BE HAPPY?

Kate Dwyer

It's all as perfect as it can be.
I'm as successful as it turns out
I'm interested in being,
with health enough to do as I like.
No one is dying, at least not this week.
The Barbarians are breaking down
doors somewhere, but not here.
I did not pay a bribe to renew my passport.
My home is warm, the lights go on.
Water always comes out of the faucet.
I needed some new socks so I bought some.
And tonight, when I'm hungry,
I'll heat that soup I made on Sunday.
I have to wonder
Why can't I just be happy?

Prompt # 22

Should You?

You Should Too (Just Sayin')

Jacquie Bellon

Hey what's up? Wow dude!
That's a good question!
I'm gluten free, vegan, freegan,
deep cleansing with
Chaparral, Burdock & Pokeroot,
and, like, I'm meditating
dude, twice a day, everyday,
after my green smoothie.
I'm in the moment,
I'm in the now,
I'm pushing the envelope,
breaking through the clutter,
for more face time,
less brain-drain-screen time,
not drinking the Kool-Aid,
eating my own dogfood.
It's a paradigm shift,
like, it's like
part of my DNA,
and dude,
you should too,
just sayin'.

Prompt #22: Should You?

SHOULD

Liz Collins

If only we could take it out
shoot it from a darkened window
it would smother guilt
on its way down
which would fall on regret
both crashing in on shame.

I will gladly hook blocks
on its haughty 'S'
throw it in the deep
I will do it now
so I can say what I couldn't
when it was alive
when it was still the Boss:
I didn't donate money
I didn't do my yoga.

Prompt #22: Should You?

Just Before I Become the Envy of Everyone I Know

Kate Dwyer

My friends are serving advice.
they pass it, hot and steaming,
across the table
with the cornbread and the baby peas.
You should go to France.
You should buy some stocks with dividends.
You should teach college
 in Montana.
You should be dating.
I should.
I would.
And I will,
Just as soon as I reconfigure
myself to match the woman
being passed about at supper.
I will go to Provence,
portfolio bulging with dividends,
fresh from my home in Missoula,
with my lovely
financially secure beau,
the one I met, teaching Amercan Lit.
And when I come home
then can we just have dinner?
Can you just pass
the cornbread,
 please?

Prompt # 23

Forget It

AGING GRACEFULLY?

Jacquie Bellon

I don't think so,
It's not for me,
know I should try.
I admire those who do, but
I hate losing friends,
losing sight, hearing, height,
so much of my strength,
hate losing words
in mid-sentence
only to have them re-appear
when I don't need them.
It's not funny,
I am not amused,
and why did it come
so soon anyway?

Prompt #23: Forget It

Three Ways to Dementia

Liz Collins

Begin softly with an orchestral suite,
a solo clarinet is just a small fact--
you knew it this morning
don't worry too much about the French horn,
the plot of the novel that floats away
on its fine pitch.
The flutes, then the cello--they could have been important
did you forget a deadline? An important name?
But no matter--let them tootle off
down their own sweet paths.

Each letting go lightens your load
the piano, the oboe section, eight violins
four bass cellos, the drums
to the crescendo;
the grand exodus of reason.

Or

let bits of knowledge follow the stream
tinkling around rocks,
sail them down river like paper boats
one at a time;
What is dark matter
What is smaller than a quark
How to make paper mâché.
They will gather twigs and branches--
Which countries have you visited
What is your password--
that sort of confusion.

Prompt #23: Forget It

The noise picks up with the volume of water
over and around rocks through bank grasses
rushing by houses through towns
through the remains of your life
to the confluence and out to sea—
the relief of it,

gone.

Or
thoughts can go
the way spring storms let loose
dark still air, a foreboding,
a feeling--
one drop of hail--
what were the directions? Then
the sudden downpour of white--
the beauty of it, separate drops melting
merging at the grate of the drain
how to make tortilla soup how
to drive the name
of your town your
husband your
children. Let it all
pour away.

Forget It

Kate Dwyer

I feel so blessed to share this time with you
Oh, forget it
I just have to post this update
No worries
shoot these two emails
it's all good
pin this photo on Pinterest
no problem
and scroll through my twitter feed.
Now, I'm all yours!
oops. Was that your phone or mine?

Prompt # 24

Collage of the Brain

A River Runs Through It

Jacquie Bellon

After days of rain
river in a
big uproar
scouring beaches
summer's trash caught
in the willows
I wish it would
run through the
wilder shores of
my complicated mind
flush the residue
stranded between synapses
let me start with
a clear beginning.

Prompt #24: Collage of the Brain

My Brain, a Mixed Media Collage

Liz Collins

I could lay it out like a map
since maps are my "thing"
and we can have a series
of dark red lines for the main roads
leading from Important Ideas
to the Center of Actual Doing.

If this were a true autobiography
of my brain, those lines would be sketchy
faded, or broken in spots
an image of my keys in the top left quadrant
with a lovely clear red line from the bottom right--
almost reaching them.

I'd paint a swath of fire engine red
from the bottom left to the top right
across the Anger Center which rubs right up
against Guilt and Envy, yellow-green variations
with a burlap texture.
Here I'd like to introduce some thick stitches
of Apathy Blue to sew it all together
and to tone down that garish green
of Distasteful Thought.

Light dry brush strokes and splatters
of pinks can signify humor
leaving some white space and gaps
since I usually blow the punch line
thanks to the broken blue map lines
showing what used to be freeways
from the Retrieval Center
but what the map now shows
as four-wheel drive.

Prompt #24: Collage of the Brain

And by the way, there's a Retrieval Rat.
He does the best he can
with the antiquated system-
ground service, rough roads
no "beam me up, Scotty"
no air traffic controller
he'll be small with whiskers askew
and tail atwitter, not knowing which way to turn

When I send him for something, like the word
"frustration"—
that being a series of pthalo blue spikes
covering the entire left half of the collage,
which is why we have
Quinocridone gold wisdom and compassion-- spirals
undulating through the whole scene peeking out
in unexpected places like next to Envy
and, more obviously just behind poor Rat.

And finally, I will whitewash the whole thing--
oh, don't worry it just puts a nice calm haze over everything
so nothing stands out too much
I call it the Spiritual Glaze
nothing is too good, nothing is too bad
everything settles together
like a winter's fog.

Prompt #24: Collage of the Brain

THINKING IN A STRAIGHT LINE

Kate Dwyer

Who does that?
As in let me think about that.
As in hang on, missy, you better think this through.
Like you start in Indianapolis
get on the interstate and go straight to Baltimore-
stopping only for gas.
Instead of getting on a two lane highway,
seeing a sign for fresh doughnuts daily
and while you're eating
you hear there's an antique show in
Louisville this weekend, so you
still head east, but really more southeast now,
and haven't you always wanted to see Cade's Cove,
that little valley in Kentucky time forgot?
Oh wait, was that Tennessee?
Kentucky and Tennessee are like two hands
folded together in a lap.
I think Brian's brother moved to Tennessee to
work for Fed Ex. We should go see him, we're so close.
Do you remember that movie with
Tom Hanks? He worked for Fed Ex. He had that friend
Wilson? Remember, the volleyball?
And then Wilson floated away? God, that was sad.

I was standing in the kitchen
with my mother,
young enough that she crouched down
to answer me eye to eye-
"When you think about something," I asked,
"do you start, and then do you think about it,
then do you stop because you're done?
In a straight line like that?"
I don't know, she said, and
I could tell she didn't.
It might be more curvy than that.
Why don't you wash your hands,
help me with these biscuits?
We'll think about that after dinner.

Prompt # 25

Crossing the Line

For Laura

Jacquie Bellon

When it happened
I said
I have a name
I have a face
and you're fucking
my husband of twenty years.
twenty years later
I thank you.

Prompt #25: Crossing the Line

Aqua Aerobics

Liz Collins

It is sweet the way they wade through the water
seeking each other out before class
like beavers embarking a project
they tiptoe to doors close off cool air
sealing us all in a chlorinated fog.

I see them every third breath
through steamy goggles
try to catch the time
stroke   stroke   stroke
breathe
see their colorful suits
stroke   stroke   stroke
breathe
their water slippers toeing the surface
it's 9 a.m.
stroke   stroke   stroke
don't overstay they will unhook the lanes
press you out.

The music starts with Here Comes the Sun
waist high in warm water arms out like stork wings
thus they begin Aqua Aerobics.

It is one of the lines I wonder
how I will cross when will I slip
from boisterous lap swimming
to this class.
I smile at them
from my pedestal of "youth"
at sixty years of age, white hair
hidden under blonde
aging body armored
with exercise.

Prompt #25: Crossing the Line

Maybe it will start with a fall
a broken hip, necessary pool recovery
the suggestion, the class, and like those
who enter hospitals and never emerge,
I will never cross back over that line
I will be tired, I will not care
I will be happy for aqua aerobics.

Prompt #25: Crossing the Line

Neighbors

Kate Dwyer

I met you once,
the day you came in response to the rental ad.
My boss is your landlord.
You liked the apartment. You moved in.
You left about the time I arrived,
you came home about the time I left each day.
Time passed. One year? Two?
My office window looks out, through
the bamboo between us, onto your front porch,
where you don't sit as you used to,
don't enjoy the tiny peace and quiet it offers.
Not that you waved or acknowledged
the lack of privacy. Both of us pretended the bamboo obscured all.
But I liked seeing someone through the leaves
resting, luxuriating, while the tribulations
of my work day pitched about me.

Towards the end of summer's last heat spell
I learned you are dying.
Not as in we are all dying in slow motion,
but as in a caretaker's car parked at the foot
of your stairs twice a week.
As in the caretaker's car parked there every day.
As in at night, when I'm going home,
a different caretaker's car arrives to take its place.
As in last week a hospital bed arrived,
then an oxygen tank while I was on break, walking the dog.

The bamboo is privacy enough now.
You won't be reading in your canvas deck chair late afternoons.
You missed the first sighting of the Sandhill Cranes last week,
All of us outside, pointing, smiling, listening to the sound of fall.
Do you know that it's fall now, and the nights are cooler
and soon the days will be too?
Do you know who your caretakers are?

Prompt #25: Crossing the Line

Do you like them? Does it matter?
Could you know that the last sweet and
difficult gift you gave anyone
is the gift you gave me, the woman who works
across the courtyard from your last home?

I wish I could
forget you are lying there, laboring for breath.
I wish I could dive deep into the
scattered bits of my life, dog walks,
dinner with friends, deadlines at work, and
not think of you at all. But I can't,
 and I thank you.

Prompt # 26

Assisted Living

Assisted Living

Jacquie Bellon

In December the rains
never stopped, days
grew dimmer,
the cats refused
to go out. One night
I stayed and slept on
the boyfriend's couch.
Seven down pillows cradled
my body into near
zero gravity under a duvet.
He kept the wood stove burning,
made morning coffee,
doctored it with more
sugar I allow myself, served it,
then went into his room.
I hibernated deep in his cave,
grew roots into comfort, light
at the flip of a switch,
just a change of clothes
while the rain kept falling.
I'm slowly waking now
to the pulse of Spring,
weeds to be pulled,
the house I used to live in—waiting.

Prompt #26: Assisted Living

Newest Arrival

Liz Collins

Cloaked in celebration
and an indigo wrap from Egypt
she steps across the threshold
Of Golden Manor Assisted Living

like a teenager in a new school
her German accent bubbles out
spreading life seeding the plain
not knowing what will sprout
and take hold

with conversation of art
ideas of wine on the deck
come summertime
her past unfolds like a favorite dress
from an old trunk.

This she is sure of;
she has not peaked that hill
just to ease down the back side
she will not dismiss the last episodes
of her riveting life just because
she has crested the last mountain
and is in her final place
she will not glide slowly to the end
she will press through the rolling remains
pushed by her past
present breezes tickling her neck
she will keep pedaling
pedaling hard to the last.

Assisted Living

Kate Dwyer

At the far end of the hall was a sitting room; two walls of windows, two round tables, five chairs, and a door to the outside. Nice light, but too far to travel for most residents, hence mostly empty. So, twice each day, one man could sit alone, eating his lunch and dinner on a tray brought by a smiling attendant. He would watch with amused detachment, as my mother passed through, headed for the closest exit to her room, dog in tow, escaping the offenses of institutional life.

"Wash your gloves." was his first offering. She was dabbing her nose with a tissue, suffering from her third cold in as many weeks. She stopped, startled after a month of his silent nods and shy smiles. But she began washing her gloves. By week six, he knew her name. "Drink more water, Gretta. You want out of here, don't you?" She most assuredly did. "You're dehydrated. I can see it from here." She began counting glasses of water each day.

Christmas afternoon, festivities spilled out into the grand foyer from the dining room. Wine was poured, roast beef was draped across plates, and holiday music jangled from speakers. Down the hall, he ate dinner at his usual solitary table. "Gretta needs some magnesium." he said, as I passed through the room on my way home from the least festive holiday meal ever. "It would make her bones stronger." OK, I said, Merry Christmas. I went home and ordered some that night.

She left at the end of January. Strong enough to shower herself, eating enough to gain weight, clear headed enough to swallow the right pills at the right times of day. We didn't see him to say goodbye. Now and then, we talk about returning for a visit. We don't. But if we did, we would go at mealtime, through the side door, at the far end of the hall.

Prompt # 27

Other Wise

Pilgrim

Jacquie Bellon

In the mountains of Tibet
we saw pilgrims
in full body prostrations
inching their way to Lhasa.
I've never done that
or walked the Camino.
My life has been
a long journey
to some sacred space.
Now life itself
is the sacred space.

Prompt #27: Other Wise

FORSYTHIA

Liz Collins

By the calendar
it's time, the light hangs around
after dark and green deepens
around your plump buds
wanting to push forth
like milk from a breast
no holding back

but hard rain beats
your scratches of yellow
day after day

and when the sun does come
will you be too tired
or will you come
like popcorn
overflowing the bowl?

Prompt #27: Other Wise

OTHER WISE

Kate Dwyer

Autumn mid-day, light breeze
a wordless command deep inside
says look up
and there
Sandhill Cranes high
and travelling southward
a tiny soundless v

Prompt # 28

Red Prairie Dawn

THE PRAIRIE

Jacquie Bellon

There's something about
that space I know
nothing about.
Driving through it
intent on getting home,
seeing nothing but the road,
I missed the whole thing.
But when friends get
that faraway look
trying to describe
the beauty, I can
almost see it
in their eyes.

Prompt #28: Red Prairie Dawn

Silence

Liz Collins

Even at 65mph barreling
down the country road
you still can be awed
by this red prairie dawn
Kansas fields and winged blackbirds
like question marks on sticks.

Slow to crunching gravel
let red dust settle
cut the engine—oh, the silence
open the door let it fill you.

Let early morning air lift the wheat
a strand of hair
a bird
stand in the space between trills
calligraphy of the meadowlark.
Hear the bounty in the void
between her notes
and in the silence

silence full
as a blossom's
bursting forth.

RED PRAIRIE DAWN

Kate Dwyer

Two thirds sky
one third land
for a thousand miles.
Endless grids of corn and soybeans,
an occasional fallow field of stubble,
trees allowed only
along the hedgerows.
It makes for a straight horizon,
a groomed and uneventful terrain.

Those skies though, those skies.
Tumbles of clouds, roiling up
in high relief, dragging hot
sheets of summer rain behind them.
Blizzards that start with
just a scattering of flakes
then so much snow
you can't tell where
sky stops and earth begins.

And most of all first dawn,
unfurling a ribbon of
luminescent mandarin orange
just above the dull grey ground,
just below the deepest violet night.

Prompt # 29

Just One Tree

Our House

Jacquie Bellon

Twenty or thirty trunks,
beetle kills all,
cut, peeled & stacked,
one tree at a time,
sat covered for years.
We bought the lot for
a thousand dollars,
squared some for corner posts,
used the rest for beams.
Mortise and Tenon
simple & strong joints
made the ancient way.
Basic bones, a skeleton
fleshed out with windows
bought second hand.
A red tile floor,
Incense Cedar ceiling,
steel roof with
a rooster weather vane
moaning in the night.
This sturdy house
facing East, the rising sun,
the river's song from
the canyon below.

Prompt #29: Just One Tree

GRANDMOTHER

Liz Collins

Lay up against her wide heart
torso and cheek alike
stretch your arms
as if to include the curve
of the world.

There's comfort there
under her rough veneer
fungal and fertile
she's more than a redwood, a fir.

Press your ear hear
the hundred years
humbly know her
inside out

finger her bark
feel her scars
the stars above
shone then as now

take a breath
she will give what you need
she will take what you give.

Just One Tree

Kate Dwyer

I drive to work
against the flow of logging trucks
coming down the hill.
Five, six fresh cut logs to a load.
Large, magnificent trunks that
yesterday, or day before, were
tall, magnificent trees.
Once, on a long straight stretch
I watched a semi hauling one single log.
A massive trunk
jammed tight between the staves.
One venerable tree from the time
of the Emancipation Proclamation,
the Transcontinental Railroad.
I slowed as it passed, pulled over,
watched it disappear down the road
in my rear view mirror;
Lincoln, on his final trip to Springfield.

Prompt # 30

Wet and Wild Spring

NINETY-SEVEN INCHES

Jacquie Bellon

It's a record now
these months of rain
after five years of drought.
Highways collapsed, rivers
became torrents, creeks, roads
became rivers,
waterfalls we had forgotten
flowed again,
mosses devoured, ran
rampant over rocks.
In April we whispered
"I've had enough" and
still it rained.
All along I wanted
the river to rip out
the bridge, the road
to slide all the way down.
taking wildflowers to new places.
I wanted it wilder, wetter
just like when I was young
sprouting breasts, hair,
new ideas and there was
no stopping it
no containing it
the green juice of
all that pulsing, that
extravagance of youth
just like now
this Spring
gorging on life.

Prompt #30: Wet and Wild Spring

AT THE WILD AND SCENIC FILM FESTIVAL
Liz Collins

Inside for most of this day
in dark rooms, glaciers
break off in 5 story pieces and
children wade in rivers of poison
earthquakes swallow paved cities.

I watch the rain
stream down tall steamy panes
outside an excitement
of raincoats and umbrellas
yet we are too thirsty to risk the words
El Nino.

Out in the cool waterlogged night
asphalt drowns
rivers spread
drains overflow.
Springs spout from hillsides
rain drums roofs, windshields,
and the impenetrable earth.
It streams down my face
over my lips, into my mouth, quenching.

My heart beats large
busting open hard-caked hope
and I try to hold it down
keep it whole and intact
and manageable, that egg of hope
but still I cup my hands under downspouts
and splash through puddles
like a child.

Prompt #30: Wet and Wild Spring

A Wet and Wild Spring

Kate Dwyer

Mid-month it rained so hard
the daffodils lay down and did not get up again.
The apple trees pelted us with blossoms;
death by wet confetti.
I emptied the rain gauge 6 times in 3 weeks.
And a sinkhole the size of a battleship
swallowed the parking lot at the tire store.
It took no prisoners.
Still, after 5 years of drought,
we dared not complain.
I put on my rain suit for the 64th day in a row
and tried to be grateful that
I would be soaked through before
the dog walk was over.

Prompt # 31

Before You Know It

GROWING OLD

Jacquie Bellon

What happened to the eyebrows?
where's the one that arched higher
over the right eye, wanting to know more?
Eyelashes are mostly gone,
lids lean heavily over,
fatigued from years of bucking up.
Mother was right about the face lifts,
hers and the ones she wished for me.
But it's too late now,
too late for the tummy tuck,
and the hair color.
I've let myself go
and landed on all fours.
I can see in the dark now,
go barefoot on gravel,
converse with animals,
sleep outside for months,
sleep alone for years.
Hoofed and horned
I pass unnoticed in a crowd

Prompt #31: Before You Know It

The Invisible Line

Liz Collins

Did I miss the finish line for youth?
Did I cross over it
somehow miss it entirely?
There should be a banner at least
because I'm still wearing that little dress
and when I look back, ok
now I see it, red letters, all caps,
and here I am in my little dress and boots
standing in line at Verizon
moving my body to Lady Gaga.

There are rules, it seems,
on this side of the line.
Should I not be dancing
at all in public?
And when my subtle swishes and taps
threaten to turn to full blown dancing
this is code red, I see,
no matter who you are.

Today I walked out of the grocery store
into the wild spray of wet weather mouthing
the word "maelstrom" just because
I'd never said aloud.
I can smear lipstick
outside the line call the cat the dog
now that I've passed the banner.

But still I pretend
to know the man calling me
from across the street
waving like he knows me well.

Prompt #31: Before You Know It

Still I pretend to remember
the movie they're talking about
or the book I finished.
That line I have yet to cross
where the pretending can halt
where I let loose the reins
and say no, I don't remember.

Prompt #31: Before You Know It

SHELF LIFE

Kate Dwyer

We used to be four retired helpers
at the farmer's market,
cheerfully greeting shoppers,
re-stocking romaine, heirlooms and kale.
Then one dropped out, then another.
Was it arthritic thumbs?
Was it shoulders, hips or low backs
that couldn't keep up?
Then this year it hit me.
It's the customer names.
From the corner of my eye I
see them coming.
I see them smiling.
They're eager to chat while they shop.
In desperation,
I reach for a flat of cucumbers
under the eggplant.
To rearrange I must face away
and bend down.
It buys me a full minute of time.
Perhaps someone will call their name
before I need to.
Maybe they're in a hurry and will move on.
I comb the alphabet-
Alice, Betsy, Corina?
Deborah, Dana, Deirdre?
Finally I stand, braced for defeat.
They're gone.
But here comes another one-
another face,
another name I won't have in time,
and only these vegetables
to protect me.

Prompt # 32

If Something Happens to Me

IF SOMETHING HAPPENS TO ME
Jacquie Bellon

Come in, feel free,
take what you want.
I have too much art,
too much jam in the pantry,
antique linen in the armoire.
Don't forget the masks
for your multiple personalities.
Pick through the journals, the books,
paintings I never sold.
When you leave
open all the doors and windows,
let the outside in
to take care of the rest.

Prompt #32: If Something Happens to Me

IF SOMETHING HAPPENS

Liz Collins

If something happens to me
life will go on, my husband
will rise in the morning
he will balance in the dark
on a leg, put a sock on
the dogs will still jump for biscuits
and he will comply
coffee will be made and drunk
the motor of business will putter and spurt
and start up again
talk will turn from somber to loud
laughter will resume.

Once, I was swallowed
by the whale of my father's dying
struggled to survive in that dark belly
when a poster stared me down;
a smiling couple throwing their grandchild
high into the cloudless blue,
the living world a trespasser
in my dark temple.

But life goes on
there is no other course,
we put one sock on
then the other.

IF SOMETHING HAPPENS TO ME

Kate Dwyer

IF something happens to me?
You mean, that last *Something*
beyond what's been happening
all along?
Beyond getting older,
less wise, less nimble,
less tall, less commanding,
more wrinkled, more grey,
more like my mother,
less like my father,
except when I'm
more like my father and
less like my mother?
Beyond being closer than I was this morning
to not even being here at all?
But enough about me. What if
something happens to you?

Prompt # 33

In the End

A Tiny Reminder

Jacquie Bellon

Already a year
into his absence
his last poem,
three lines, red ink,
a tiny reminder.

Prompt #33: In the End

IN THE END

Liz Collins

Sometimes I still feel it in a flash
when everything was rich and joyous
cadmium yellow straight from the tube
it's like time stopped on a Saturday morning
and there is my father with fresh
donuts, their jelly the color of hydrangea
and there is the whole blue sea wanting me
like it could wait no longer.

Mostly days wash over me
in mere hints of color
and it is not about happiness
or lack of it
but I can't help
but compare it with the pure
pigment of youth.

In the end, I imagine a wide brush
whitewashing days, flattening the landscape
blending me into the background
a blue grey haze, a streak,
the final upturned stroke.

In the End

Kate Dwyer

He got the girl
and never looked back,
peace reigned,
the black rhinoceros returned
from the brink of extinction,
they came to the table and
resolved their differences,
we all prospered at our passions,
the native people regained their homelands,
the car started right up,
your cancer was cured,
we lived long and happily
and died in our sleep.

About the Poets

Jacquie Bellon lives in a house she built by hand with ex-husband #3. The view is excellent. The place and community of the San Juan Ridge has inspired much of her obsessions and life work in art and writing.

Kate Dwyer was born and raised in east central Illinois. Even after 30+ years of life in the Sierra Foothills her sensible Midwestern protestant psyche seems, for better or worse, solidly intact. Professionally, she divides her time between business coaching and running a small jewelry manufacturing company. She writes in the margins.

Liz Collins graduated from the University of Colorado with a BFA and currently makes her living as a fine artist. Her poetry and short stories have been published in *The Raven's Perch*, *Earth's Daughters* and *Harbinger Magazine*. She has just completed her first novel, taking place in the Blue Ridge Mountains. She resides in the foothills of the Sierra Mountains in Northern California.

www.ingramcontent.com/pod-product-compliance
Lightning Source LLC
Chambersburg PA
CBHW021956290426
44108CB00012B/1095